Modern HTML Email

Building Robust, Responsive, and Effective HTML Email

Jason Rodriguez

Written & Designed by Jason Rodriguez
Published by Two Daughters

ISBN-10: 0615863620
ISBN-13: 978-0615863627

Table of Contents

For my wife and two daughters.

Introduction

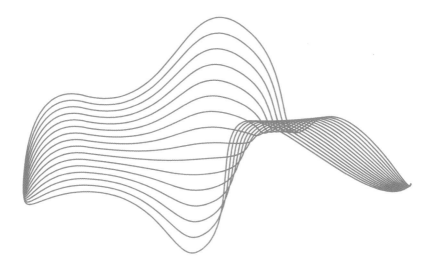

There are thousands of screen sizes, with new devices being released all the time. It's impractical to design multiple builds for each platform or form factor. Responsive design offers us a single-code-base solution that will still be compatible with whatever is coming down the pipe in six months.

Anna Yeaman
STYLECampaign

There are two jokes in the web design community. The first one goes like this:

A web designer walks into a bar and immediately leaves in disgust upon noticing all of the tables.

And here is the second:

HTML Email.

It is a widely held view among web professionals that HTML email is a joke - something to be laughed at and looked down upon. Email marketing is often derided as outdated, tacky, and more trouble than it's worth, which is sad because email marketing consistently yields a higher return on investment than most other marketing avenues. And in comparison to marketing on social media channels, there is hardly a contest – email marketing gets better results, period.

Most of the derision stems from two sources - the outdated technology used to build emails and the poor design that most marketing emails exhibit. There is both good and bad news here. The bad news is that both sources of derision are accurate. The good news is that things are changing.

Recent years have seen an influx of new techniques, such as responsive design, applied to HTML emails. And many companies and designers are tackling email marketing with an enthusiasm never before seen in the industry.

Nearly every week, I find myself both surprised and delighted by some of the emails that hit my inbox. I have seen campaigns that rival even the best-designed websites for aesthetics and content. The short-form

---

nature of email allows both designers and content-producers to focus on the core of their messages - and to find a beautiful and creative way to deliver them.

But building great emails that perform across the myriad of clients and devices is difficult and, oftentimes, extraordinarily frustrating. Email designers have more than just a few different browsers to worry about - and we don't have the luxury of the latest JavaScript library to ease our pain. Building emails is a trying, confusing, and usually dirty practice. It involves working with markup at which most designers would cringe and hacking your way to success.

I have dealt with these frustrations over the course of a few years of sending a lot of emails. I have seen what works, and, perhaps more importantly, what does not work. This book is my attempt to guide both new and experienced designers in the right direction when building modern responsive emails.

What to Expect

The first section of this guide – **The Mechanics of HTML Email** – will help to explain some of the underpinnings of email marketing. It briefly discusses topics such as how HTML emails are sent, the role of email service providers, permissions, types of campaigns, and legal considerations. Though not much space is dedicated to these subjects in this book, it is important to grasp these basics to keep your campaigns on the right track.

The second section of the book – **Designing Modern Email** - focuses on some of the initial planning and aesthetic choices you will need to consider before working on the actual coding of your emails. It touches on things like typography, layouts, and mobile considerations.

The third section – **Building Modern Email** – is the heart of the book. It walks you through building a robust, responsive email newsletter and discusses the thinking behind many of the decisions that go into coding. This section is filled with examples so you have an opportunity to see a lot of code, as well as several common problems and their solutions.

The fourth section – **Optimizing for Effectiveness** – deals with things you can do to make your campaigns as effective as possible. It discusses testing your campaign, tracking email metrics, optimizing for the inbox, and getting readers to actually read and interact with your emails.

This book takes a fairly opinionated look at modern email. It is not an in-depth discussion of every possible technique for creating email campaigns, but it will cover what I believe to be some of the more important ones. At the end of the book you will find a reference section with many of the resources I used while writing this book, as well as in my day-to-day work as an email designer. I thoroughly recommend that you check out these resources for more information regarding some of the opinions and techniques that I touch upon in this book.

A Quick Note

This book contains code. Due to the limitations of the book format, the code has necessarily been formatted and taken out of the context of a full email template.

I have tried to make it as readable as possible. Where the code snippet has been removed from it's context, I have used a pink ellipsis to denote the missing context. Here is an example:

```
. . .
<tr>
  <span>This snippet is out of context.</span>
</tr>
. . .
```

Any code or tags mentioned within the text are set in a monospace font. Here is an example `img` tag mentioned in the text.

I highly recommend downloading the full email template available at http://resources.modernhtmlemail.com.

The Mechanics
of HTML Email

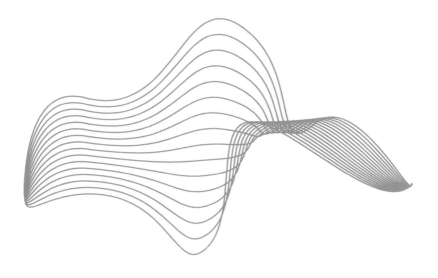

Overview

Chances are that if you bought this guide, then you are already working in the email industry or soon will be. Maybe you are part of a seasoned team of designers doing high-volume sends for a multi-national corporation, or perhaps you are the sole designer in a small agency tasked with starting up a client's new email strategy, or maybe you are just a single designer freelancing and helping small businesses improve their digital presence. In any case, it is important to understand some of the logistics that underpin email marketing.

There is a lot that goes into actually sending out an email campaign apart from the design, copy, and code. From IT considerations to legal compliance, there are several moving pieces that ultimately determine how successful your email campaign will be. Let's take a look at the most important.

How Email Is Delivered

The most basic thing to understand about email marketing is that it is a different beast than sending your best friend a message through one of your accounts. HTML email marketing requires a number of IT considerations to be successful, and getting any one of these parts wrong can ruin your day - and more importantly, your relationship with both your clients and subscribers.

When I talk about email marketing, I am talking about sending "multipart-alternative" messages to a subscriber list that has been collected through legal channels. The "multipart-alternative" message type bundles both a plain-text and an HTML version of a message for delivery. It wraps both versions for delivery with the appropriate headers so that ISPs and email providers can identify the message and deal with it accordingly.

It is important that all the infrastructure underlying this process is properly set up to ensure delivery. If your mail transfer agent (which bundles the message), server, domains, or IP addresses are improperly configured, many ISPs or email providers will block your emails from delivering. A poor infrastructure can also lead to your messages being blocked by spam filters and your domains getting blacklisted by email providers or corporate firewalls. These outcomes are equally terrible and should be avoided at all costs.

Fortunately, there are dozens of companies out there that handle all of that geeky stuff for you. These companies are called Email Service Providers (ESPs), and they soothe a lot of the pain traditionally associated with email marketing.

Email service providers handle all of the IT needs associated with email marketing. This includes managing servers and IP addresses, registering and reporting on bounces, unsubscribes, and spam complaints, and providing tools to both register subscribers and manage them throughout the lifecycle of their subscription. Most ESPs offer even more services, like advanced reporting, customer management, and custom account and server solutions for high-volume senders.

Some of the best ESPs are Campaign Monitor, MailChimp, Emma, ExactTarget, and Constant Contact.

Campaign Monitor

Campaign Monitor is one of the leading email service providers.

.Vhile the services provided by ESPs may seem pricey, the cost is reasonable considering the time and effort that would be associated with running your own servers for email marketing. The main takeaway is that with HTML email marketing, you are sending a message in two parts - plain text and HTML. It's on you to make sure both parts are well-made and safely and reliably sent to your subscribers.

Understanding Permissions

Apart from the content of your email campaign, permissions are the single most important part of email marketing. If you screw up the permissions of your list, you're going to have a bad time.

There are very few cases in which you do not actually need a user's permission to send them an email. Even in those cases, it is a good practice to get the user's permission anyway. For our purposes, let's just go ahead and assume that you need to get a subscriber's permission before sending to them.

An example email sign up form.

There are two methods to obtaining a user's permission. These methods are known as the **single opt-in** method and the **double**

---

opt-in or **confirmed opt-in** method. Both start out the sam̲e̲
with someone deliberately adding their email address to a list — a
form on your website, a form on one of your social networks, or in
person. For the single opt-in method, no further action is required on
the part of the user before you can start sending emails. However, the
double opt-in method requires an intermediate step before you can
start sending emails. This step usually takes the form of you sending an
email with a confirmation link that the user must click to confirm their
subscription.

Before deciding on a method of collecting subscribers, it is important
to understand the benefits and drawbacks of both methods. Let's start
with the single opt-in method.

It is generally easier to grow your subscriber list using the single opt-
in method than the double opt-in method. Because there are no extra
steps in the single opt-in process, it is easy for subscribers to quickly
sign up and start receiving emails. Though single opt-in subscriber
lists tend to grow more quickly and end up larger than double opt-in
subscriber lists, the single opt-in method is not without flaws. A major
drawback of using the single opt-in method is that there is a fair chance
that a significant percentage of the subscribers will have entered bad
email addresses, or may not even be real people to begin with. By
failing to confirm the email addresses submitted by subscribers, you
may find yourself sending to bots and bad email addresses, which will
lead to high bounce rates and a poor sending reputation.

It is not as easy to grow your subscriber list using the double opt-in
method. Because there is an extra step required of the subscribers,
your subscriber list will probably grow at a slower rate and likely
be smaller than if you used the single opt-in method as a result of
subscribers failing to follow through with the confirmation step.

---

however, this smaller list is not necessarily a drawback. At least in theory, the subscriber list generated using the double opt-in method should be cleaner and more responsive to your marketing efforts. The thinking is that because the subscribers actively confirmed their subscriptions, they are more likely to pay attention to and act on your campaigns than the passive subscribers on a single opt-in list.

Traditionally, the accepted best practice is the double opt-in method. However, many subscribers and email marketers have recently expressed a preference for the single opt-in method. This is likely because the single opt-in method eases the burden of confirmation on the subscriber's end and ensures quicker list growth on the marketer's end. Email Wizardry's Nicole Merlin expresses this view:

> I really hate having to double opt-in for mailing lists. I wish unscrupulous people didn't exist so that we wouldn't have to do it.
>
> ## Nicole Merlin
> Email Wizardry *via Twitter*

When determining which of the two methods to employ in your email campaigns, the most important factor to consider is your targeted audience. If you are marketing to a narrow segment, chances are that you can safely use the single opt-in method without worrying too much about subscribers submitting bad email addresses. If people are interested in a niche market, then they will likely more readily (and accurately) give out their email addresses, which will lead to a nice, clean subscriber list. On the other hand, if you are working in a massive industry and collecting subscribers via a heavily trafficked website, the double opt-in method is probably the way to go. Requiring subscribers to actively confirm their subscription will help weed out the bots and bad email addresses that will likely be submitted in such an environment and result in a cleaner subscriber list. Basically, determining which method to use is a numbers game. The likelihood of a subscriber list being clean decreases as the list grows, so if you believe your means of collecting email addresses will result in a large yield, it is probably best to employ the double opt-in method.

There is another way to obtain a subscriber list, but I did not include it above as one of the methods for obtaining permissions because I would never recommend it. This means of obtaining subscribers is renting or buying an email subscriber list. There are several places that market and sell huge subscriber lists, but it is never worth purchasing one. The subscribers on these lists opted into something, but the thing they opted into was not your list. Chances are that such lists were illegally harvested and are extremely unreliable. If you start marketing to one of these lists, don't be surprised by how many emails bounce and how quickly your sender reputation nosedives.

Finally, it is important to keep in mind that even if you have a good list and explicit permission from subscribers, you still need to keep that list warm. It is key to actively engage your list so the subscribers do not forget who you are. There is a fine balance you need to maintain: on the one hand, you don't want to over-send and risk being labeled spam; on the other hand, you don't want to send so infrequently that subscribers forget they gave you permission and mark you as spam. A good rule of thumb in ensuring that your list is warm is to send an email at least every few months. I've seen some people claim that a list has up to 18 months before it should be considered cold, but I strongly disagree. Do you remember signing up to a newsletter more than a month or two after it happened? I didn't think so. If you haven't sent an email to your list in a few months, it has grown cold.

ize that you have allowed a list to go cold, a good practice out a campaign to renew your subscribers' permissions. The software company Panic does an excellent job of this. It sends out reminders of how you got on its subscriber list along with an easy way to confirm your interest in continuing to receive emails.

Cleaning ? up list!

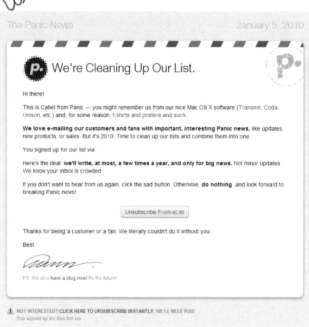

Software developer Panic gives cold subscribers the option of opting out. This keeps their lists clean and emails highly targeted.

Employing a practice such as Panic's is key to both keeping subscribers happy and keeping subscriber lists clean, particularly when you only occasionally send to your subscriber list.

In addition to obtaining permission from your subscribers, you must also be aware of the law surrounding email marketing and the ways in which your emails may be marked as spam. These considerations are explored in the following sections.

Legal Considerations

Chances are that you work for a U.S.-based company or are sending on behalf of one. If you are, then any commercial email marketing (i.e., most of the stuff you will be sending) is subject to certain legal requirements set out in the **CAN-SPAM Act of 2003** and enforced by the Federal Trade Commission. Europeans have a similar set of requirements outlined in the **EU Opt-in Directive of 2003**. Even if these laws do not apply to you, I recommend that you take note of their underlying principles because they are excellent practices to follow, regardless of whether or not they are required.

The CAN-SPAM Act and EU Opt-In Directive are filled with nuances that you should probably read at some point. For the purposes of this book, I have focused on the key rules that you must follow in order to be in compliance with these laws. These key rules are summarized below:

Do not use misleading header information. Do not lie in your headers, "From", "Reply-To", or "To" fields. Just like in life, you need to be honest about who you are.

Do not use misleading information in your subject lines. Do not try to trick people into opening an email by using a misleading subject line. The subject line must be directly related to the content of the email.

Identify your email as an advertisement or marketing material. There is no hard and fast rule as to how to accomplish this, but it must be clear that your email is of a commercial nature. In many cases, the content takes care of this for you - but when in doubt, spell it out for your subscribers.

Give a physical address. A valid physical address for whoever is initiating the sending of the email must be included in the email. It used to be a requirement that a business lists its brick-and-mortar address, but changes to the law have made it acceptable to use P.O. boxes and private mailboxes through a third-party. This is awesome news for individuals that want to send out marketing emails without disclosing their home address.

Give an obvious - and working - way to opt out of emails. Do not try to trick people by hiding the method for unsubscribing from your emails.

Make the means of unsubscribing clear and make sure it works. The best practice is to make unsubscribing as simple as possible. Also, the law requires that the method of unsubscribing is functional for at least 30 days after the email is sent.

When people opt out, honor their request within ten days. When a subscriber provides their email address and the clearly stated intention of opting out, it is your responsibility to remove them from your subscriber list within ten days.

Even if someone else handles your email marketing – you must monitor what they are doing on your behalf. You can't just pass the buck. Both you and whoever handles email marketing on your behalf are legally responsible for what is sent and must comply with the applicable laws.

It is also important to note what the CAN-SPAM Act does not explicitly regulate. One such thing is how you may gather permissions. The CAN-SPAM Act does not require a sender to get explicit permission before sending marketing emails so long as the sender adheres to the guidelines above. Also, certain types of emails are exempt from the CAN-SPAM Act – specifically transactional emails, religious and political messages, and any sort of national security message.

Finally, I should mention that the CAN-SPAM Act is not widely enforced. However, I would still be careful not to slack on any of its requirements because it only takes one persistent recipient to make your job a hell of a lot less enjoyable. Fines for not following the requirements of the CAN-SPAM Act are hefty and are usually per recipient - which means they can add up quickly. It is simply not worth it to disregard these rules. And while the FTC may not consistently enforce these guidelines, many email service providers do check to make sure you are compliant. The best idea is to always strive for compliance, regardless of what you are sending.

Do Not Spam

OK, so you've got a handle on how emails are sent and the legal requirements for sending them. Before we jump into designing emails, let's talk a little bit about spam and how to avoid your emails earning a spam label.

Even if you have followed the rule of law to the T, there is still a good chance that what you send will be perceived as spam. You won't incur any fines from the FTC if your emails are merely perceived as spam, but you will likely run afoul of the rules of your ESPs and ISPs and, more importantly, irritate or not even reach your subscribers.

There is a lot you can do to avoid being perceived as a spammer. Every ESP and ISP has a different set of rules for what they consider spam. The general rule is that if it looks like spam, it will be considered spam - regardless of how well it complies with commercial laws. So how can you avoid having a message that looks like spam? Try following these basic guidelines:

AVOID USING ALL CAPS. This is a huge trigger for most spam filters and firewalls. Not only will it make your message look like spam but your readers will think you're yelling at them. Nobody likes that.

Don't mention money or deals too much. While talk of offers is necessary for many campaigns, heavy use of phrases like "deals" or "half-off" are usually indicators of a spam message.

Avoid using lots of exclamation points!!!!!! Just like with using all caps, an overuse of exclamation points is not only annoying, but also a huge trigger for spam filters.

Don't use too many images. Spammers like to hide their messages from spam filters by putting them in images, so too many images will often set off an alarm in spam filters. It should also be noted that if you rely on too many images your subscribers will likely never see your message because most email clients disable images by default.

Don't use one large image. This is an extension of the last guideline. In fact, a single large image is an even better indicator that a message is spam than too many images. Thus, having a healthy mix of text and images is a good idea. When in doubt, err on the side of using

---

text instead of images when possible.

Again, while these are not hard and fast rules, they are well-established guidelines that will help you avoid most spam filters and firewalls. And though some clients or branding guidelines may require you to break these self-imposed rules sometimes, I recommend sticking to them as much as possible.

Remember that your reputation and the relevancy of your message are the two keys to success in email marketing. Keep your reputation clean by following the laws and guidelines above. Remain relevant to your subscribers by keeping your lists warm and sending meaningful content. If you can manage this, your only concern is designing and coding a killer email.

One of the biggest problems in email marketing is assuming that your subscribers will willingly read absolutely everything you have to say. It's much easier to hit delete than to read a dull essay, so put your all into keeping your message on point and engaging.

Ros Hodgekiss
Campaign Monitor

The hardest part about designing mobile emails is predicting how a user will experience the email. Will they be opening it while watching TV, commuting to work, or just to get rid of the notification on their phone? This is why creating a consistent and coherent user experience benefits a long term email campaign.

Mobile optimisation is more than just scaling an email down to the width of a mobile phone; you need to think about how a user will see and experience every different aspect of the email. If a user at any point has trouble reading or clicking on your email then it's not working how it should be.

Alex Ilhan
eMosaic

Designing
Modern Email

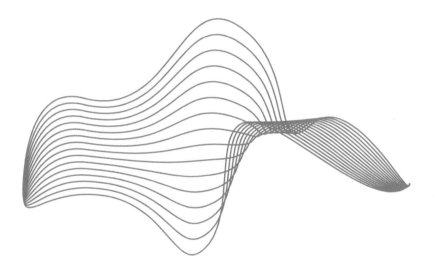

Overview

A successful email marketing campaign requires three things: a good subscriber list, a well-designed email, and excellent content. The previous sections discussed handling permissions and avoiding spamming tactics, both of which help to ensure a good list of attentive subscribers. This section focuses on how to hone your content and how to design an effective email.

I won't be digging into any code just yet. Instead I will begin by discussing some of the theory behind successful email campaigns and the considerations you should keep in mind when designing a modern email campaign.

Purpose

For most marketers, email campaigns exist to drive sales, click-throughs, and page views. That makes sense from a business perspective, but what if we redefined the purpose of email marketing? And what if, by redefining the purpose of email marketing, we not only drove those same goals, but also built a stronger, more loyal audience?

The purpose of an email campaign can be redefined by looking at it not merely as an opportunity to sell, but also as an opportunity to build a relationship with your audience. I am not advocating doing away with advertising in email campaigns, but, instead trying to get you to view your email campaigns from the perspective of your audience with the goal of providing value to that audience. If you can maximize the value provided to your audience through your email campaigns, your marketing efforts will likely be more successful than if your email campaigns are focused solely on advertising your product or driving your sales.

The best way to build a relationship with your audience is by valuing their time and rewarding their attention. Remember that they have reached out to hear more from you by signing up to be a part of your subscriber list. You should work as hard as you can to reward them in turn. While you don't always need to have a killer coupon or offer in your email, all of your content should be of great value to your audience.

Author and app developer Nathan Barry sets an excellent example of building a strong marketer-subscriber relationship. All of his emails are packed with content that is both informative and relevant to his audience. Whether it's his musings on new ways to build apps and write books, or a sample chapter from an upcoming release, he is constantly giving his subscribers something that is worth their time. When he finally does try to make a sell, he does so in a personal manner. His emails always feel like a friend suggesting an amazing product instead of an impersonal corporation jamming an ad down your throat.

There are a lot of things you can do in your emails to show that you value your audience's time. Great content is the core of the marketer-subscriber relationship. Here are a few more ideas to help grow that relationship and redefine the purpose of your campaigns:

Personalize your messages. Most email service providers make this simple to implement with hooks to add a subscriber's name to the message. You should go one step further and reference where your relationship with the subscriber stems from in the email. A gentle reminder up front of why a subscriber is getting that email or where they signed up helps avoid confusion and keeps the experience fresh in the subscriber's mind. If you are marketing products, keeping track of what a subscriber has purchased in the past and tailoring your email content to their interests is another exceptional way to personalize messages. These tactics show your subscribers you remember them and value every interaction you have with them.

Don't hit them with an ad right away. While it is understood that email marketing is just that - marketing – try to place the advertisement portion of your message later in the email if possible. For example, an agency or individual sending out campaigns may want to let its subscribers know about some cool news that might interest them before mentioning its products. Something like this won't always be an option, but it is a good way to add value to your campaigns when you can swing it.

Give your subscribers something in the email. This is probably the best way to show your subscribers that you value their time just as much as your own agenda. Pointing them to a helpful article you know they won't want to miss, giving away a sample chapter to your new book, or providing a coupon code for your service are a few examples of things of value you can include in your emails. It is no secret that people love free and exclusive stuff, so giving what you can will only help your long-term marketing goals.

Ask for feedback. Why not use some of your email campaigns to solicit feedback from your subscribers? Most people love sharing their opinions, and with it being easier than ever to set up quick surveys online, it is not a bad idea to try to collect those opinions. Asking for feedback shows that you value your subscribers' opinions and helps you to build that all-important marketer-subscriber relationship, while at the same time allowing you an opportunity to improve your product.

I am sure you can think of more ways to augment the purpose of your email marketing beyond just selling stuff. And while I know that not all campaigns and companies can get away with ideas like these all the time, any campaign focused on strengthening the marketer-subscriber relationship is a worthwhile campaign. I believe that once you redefine the purpose of your email marketing campaigns to include building a relationship with your subscribers instead of merely advertising to them, you will start to see your long-term marketing goals not only met, but also exceeded.

The most important part for us is the message. It's easy to get lost in the pursuit of the perfect layout and design, but you should always come back to the message - what are you communicating with people and what do you expect them to do? If you can nail that, everything else falls into place.

Elliot Ross
Action Rocket

ut

Once you have defined the purpose of your email you need to figure out the best way to present your message.

Just like in web design, email designs come in a variety of layouts. While you can technically layout an email however you want, most email marketing relies on a few tried and true layouts. If you browse some of the templates that most ESPs provide, you will see the same few regularly cropping up.

Let's take a look at a few of these and see how they work and in what situations you might consider using them.

The most common type of email campaign is a **multi-column** marketing campaign. These are the emails you usually see from the big brands and online sellers. They generally start with what's known as a "hero image" - something to grab the attention of users - and then break down into sections heavy with imagery and calls to action.

I would wager that the majority of marketing campaigns use some variation of this layout. Traditionally, these types of layouts are very effective in a desktop environment because image- and content-heavy emails are best viewed on large screens. The problem is that, in an age where mobile traffic is growing, these multi-column, image-heavy emails can be a burden on subscribers.

If a multi-column email isn't optimized for mobile, then most subscribers will see either a scaled down version of the email that is difficult to read and requires effort to accurately tap on CTAs, or an unscaled version that requires tedious amounts of both horizontal and vertical scrolling. While this type of unscaled display cannot be avoided

A multi-column email layout.

in some email clients (I'm looking at you, Gmail on Android), for most other clients you can, and should, try your best to optimize the experience of viewing your email on a mobile device.

Another issue with multi-column, image-heavy emails is that they require a subscriber to download and render a large number of images. As you can imagine, this is hardly a problem on a desktop. However, with the cost of data plans on mobile devices, it can greatly affect your campaigns on mobile devices. Subscribers viewing your email on a mobile device will likely not bother downloading the images used in your campaign and, if frustrated enough, may unsubscribe from future emails. This failure of mobile readers to download your images can also affect your metrics. Some metrics, like open rates, require a subscriber to download and display images for an open to be registered. If mobile readers aren't doing that, then your metrics can be greatly skewed, which may lead to some poor decision-making on your end.

An alternative to using a multi-column layout, and one that I highly recommend, is using a **single-column** layout.

Single-column layouts are typically easier and faster to build and, more importantly, require less effort to make responsive than multi-column layouts. Since you don't have to worry about rearranging and resizing multiple columns, implementing a responsive single-column template is relatively easy to do. It mainly consists of making your email fluid and adjusting the text and image sizes in the email, which I will discuss later.

An added bonus is that single-column layouts tend to force you to streamline your content. Text and image-heavy single-columns layouts can quickly get too long and require lots of scrolling for subscribers. With attention spans always in decline, long single-column emails risk not being read. To ensure that your message gets across to subscribers, it is important to keep it succinct and relevant. Single-column layouts are great at forcing you to whittle down your message to its essence.

Practically speaking, though, most companies are reluctant to adopt a

A single-column email layout.

single-column approach. A lot of thinking favors cramming as much as possible into an email and a multi-column layout is ideal for this. Also, if you know your audience is primarily made up of desktop users, then a single-column layout could require a lot of unnecessary scrolling. A good rule of thumb is to rely on multi-column emails for content and image-heavy emails and single-columns emails for shorter, text-based emails. I encourage you to mix both types of layouts and experiment with variations. You will see a lot of different layouts in use and no one style is the right style. It is ultimately up to you to assess the needs of your email campaign and its likely audience and design accordingly.

Mobile First or Desktop?

There has been a lot of debate in the web design world about whether you should build for mobile or desktop first. Camps on both sides have valid arguments, but I think it breaks down to this simple rule: know your audience and let that knowledge guide your decisions.

As with most of the other decisions regarding your email campaigns, your choice of whether to build your emails for mobile devices and then optimize for desktop viewing or build your emails for desktop and then optimize for mobile viewing should be driven by your audience, i.e., the people actually subscribing to your emails. It is probable that your email campaigns are directed to specific markets, and it is also probable that the subscribers in those specific markets lean toward certain computer tendencies. For example, if you are marketing an app for iOS then chances are good that subscribers in your targeted market check their email more often on their iPhones than on desktops. In such a situation, I would recommend using a mobile-first strategy and tailoring your design and code to look best in Apple's Mail app. On the other hand, if you are marketing a business product, I'd wager that most of your audience will be using some version of Microsoft Outlook or, unfortunately, Lotus Notes. Both of those clients typically have pretty severe issues with rendering email, so, in such a situation, I would recommend focusing your energy on building a robust desktop-friendly email that looks great in those particular clients.

In a perfect world, all campaigns would be as clear-cut as the above examples. However, I recognize that this is not the case. For example, if you are marketing for a large retailer or a product that attracts customers from all walks of life, you will need to cover a huge range of email clients. In such a situation, your best bet is to build a desktop-friendly email that works well across all clients (or as many clients as possible), and then adapt it to mobile devices as best you can. If you build a good template, this shouldn't be too much trouble.

Typography and Images

The content of your email campaign is made up of two things – type and images. Before you start coding, you need to consider your choices in typography and how to handle images.

When working on the web, designers have a huge variety of typefaces from which to choose thanks to recent browser improvements and advances from companies like TypeKit and Fontdeck, which have allowed web designers to reach levels of typographic bliss normally found only in print. Unfortunately for email designers, most of these services rely on technology that is not supported by most email clients. Thus, whereas web designers can rely on JavaScript and @ font-face support to employ the typography that suits their fancy, email designers are stuck with the old standbys of Arial, Georgia, Verdana, and a few others.

A typical font-stack for emails looks something like this:

```
style="font-family: arial, sans-serif;"
style="font-family: georgia, serif;"
```

I am sure a few of you are thinking that there is an obvious solution to this problem: just use images to compose the entirety of your message

- after all, if you just slice up your design from Photoshop, you can use any damned font you please. While that is technically true, it does not mean that composing an email entirely of images is a good idea. It is important to keep in mind that nearly all email clients disable images by default. That means that unless a subscriber has opted to display images, he will never see any of your message, including that beautiful type of yours. From a content standpoint, this is a huge problem.

Here are two pieces of advice to help you avoid this problem. First, keep the essential part of your message text rather than an image. Second, if you must display important content as an image, provide good alt-text so subscribers who have not opted to display images can still grasp what your email is about. A good practice is to style that alt-text so your email maintains its design even when images are not enabled. I will discuss how to do that when we start looking at code. When it comes to typography, the bottom line is that it is generally better to stick with the old standbys that are supported by email clients than to try to "solve" the problem of not being able to use the fancy typography of your choice by forcing all of your content into images.

A quick note on text size: Some mobile devices, like the iPhone, automatically increase the size of text if it is below 13px. You need to keep this in mind when designing your emails. If you have text smaller than 13px and don't specifically override the iPhone's behavior, then your design will likely break or render poorly. You should always explicitly declare font-sizes, so why not make your text larger than 13px from the outset?

As indicated in the discussion regarding typography above, you should try your hardest to keep the number of images in your emails to a minimum. The most obvious reason for this is that you want as much of your content as possible to be readable even when images are disabled. Another reason is that spam filters take into account how images are used within emails. Most filters look at the ratio of images versus text, and give emails a higher spam rating if that ratio is skewed in favor of images. The reasoning behind this is that a lot of spammers try to bypass filters by hiding their messages within images - something that is difficult for computers to parse. So if a spam filter sees an email that uses a high number of images or one very large image, it will score that email accordingly, which may result in the email being marked as spam.

When it comes to images, size is another important consideration. In fact, it is becoming more and more important as more and more subscribers start using their mobile devices as their primary inboxes. Data plans are expensive, and forcing your subscribers to download a lot of large images will only serve to annoy them. Generally, an annoyed subscriber is a subscriber no more, so try to keep your file sizes down. There are a ton of tools available for all platforms that can help you out with this. You will find my recommendations for which of these tools to use at the end of this guide.

As far as image formats go, I recommend sticking to JPEGS and GIFs. More and more people are using PNGs for images to take advantage of their support for transparency. However, I do not recommend regularly using PNGs due to compatibility issues with older clients. That being said, if you know you can rely on PNG support, then by all means use PNGs – just make sure you know which clients your subscribers are using and whether or not they provide support for PNGs before making the choice to use them.

Another consideration when it comes to images is whether background images should be used in your email design. There are mixed feelings in the email community when it comes to this topic. Some people believe background images should never be used because support for them across email clients is a mixed bag at best. Others believe background images can enhance your emails. Personally, I believe that background images can be wildly useful, particularly in responsive designs. For example, there is a cool technique you can use to swap out images using background images to create some really great mobile emails. If you decide to use background images, I recommend setting a fallback background color and making sure your design and message does not completely fall apart in clients that lack support for background images.

Finally, a word about what is considered the holy grail of email marketing: **video in email**. Email marketers have long sought a good, reliable means of playing videos in their campaigns – sadly without any real success. Due to the variety of clients, lack of support for plugins and JavaScript, and a wide range of video file formats and codecs, there is no reliable way to feed your subscribers your latest viral marketing message. That being said, you do not have to completely give up on the idea of including video in your email campaigns.

There are currently two ways to kind of get video emails working. The first is using animated GIFs, which allow you to fake video emails with a few caveats. First, the "videos" won't have sound. Second, GIFs can get huge fast, so you need to watch your file size, especially if you are targeting mobile devices. And third, a lot of clients do not support animated GIFs, so your subscribers will either only see the first frame in your GIF (which is not necessarily a bad thing) or nothing at all. It is for these reasons I recommend that if you choose to use animated GIFs, you do so as a flourish in your email. Don't try slapping a two-minute product demo in there. Some of the best campaigns that use animated GIFs do so in very subtle ways, such as through simple animations that draw your eyes to a particular spot in the email.

The second way to kind of get video emails to work is using HTML5 Video. It takes advantage of HTML5's new `video` tag to insert a video into your email much like an img tag inserts an image into your email. The cool thing is that in some clients this actually works. In most, though, the video is either not displayed or won't play, resulting in your subscribers only seeing the first frame. Support for HTML5 video may grow in the future, and if you can get away with using it for your audience, have at it. For now though, my recommendation to most marketers is to steer clear of video in emails.

As always, consider your audience and their capabilities when tailoring your email campaigns and making decisions regarding the design of your emails. While it is often better to play it safe in email marketing, if your audience is a specific niche and you know you can get away with some of the cooler stuff, have fun!

Navigation Patterns

While thinking about navigation for HTML emails is not always necessary, it may require consideration in some cases. For example, many retailers like to have navigation that mimics their websites. Also, in content-heavy newsletters, providing in-email navigation is helpful for subscribers.

The key to navigation is incorporating it in a way that works on mobile devices. In her excellent video on Responsive Email Design, STYLECampaign's Anna Yeaman notes the following five navigation patterns commonly used in responsive emails:

Wrap simply wraps navigation items down on lines as the screen width shrinks. This method is easy to implement, but, in certain cases, can look messy.

Stack makes navigation items 100% wide and stacks them vertically. Because this method can take up a good deal of vertical space early in the email, Anna suggests reserving it for the footer of the email, and, in most cases, I agree.

Shift takes existing navigation on the desktop view and shifts it into place in the mobile view without reorganizing or resizing the navigation items. Use caution when employing this method because it only really works with a few navigation items.

Reduce is similar to shift, except, in addition to shifting the navigation items, it also reduces the number of items in a larger navigation bar to only the most essential items in the mobile view. This is a great method for prioritizing, but stubborn clients often refuse to get rid of anything that can be clicked on.

Toggle takes the desktop navigation and hides it on mobile devices, only revealing it when toggled by a button or text link, then dismissing it again when prompted. This method is brilliant if implemented correctly, but is usually the hardest of the five methods to get working across email clients.

Again, not every email campaign will require you to consider a navigation pattern. In fact, there is much to be said about making your campaigns shorter and more succinct. With that said, it is important to understand what solutions are out there in case a client has a need for navigation. If you decide to implement any of the techniques above, make sure you test, test, test.

Early on there were lots of technical challenges, as each project brought a new design pattern we'd not tried before.

More recently trying to implement a toggle navigation was a hard technical challenge. There's obviously no JavaScript support and even when we had pure CSS builds that worked in the browser, links and show/hide states wouldn't work reliably. It's easy to get hacks like the toggle 95% of the way there, but getting them to a deployable state is tough and sometimes impossible.

Anna Yeaman
STYLECampaign

Buttons and Calls to Action

Buttons and Calls to Action (from now on CTAs) are the meat and potatoes of every email marketing campaign. Their purpose is to direct subscribers to the places marketers want them to go. That is why, for clients of email designers, buttons and CTAs are usually the most important aspects of an email.

When designing your buttons and CTAs in the age of mobile, you should keep a couple things in mind. First, and most importantly, is the size of your button or CTA. Apple gives the guideline of 44px square when developing touch applications for iOS, and that is a good place to start when thinking about your buttons. The idea is to make sure that your buttons are neither too narrow nor too short. Essentially, if your thumb cannot successfully tap your buttons, you should consider resizing. Second is how people hold their devices. A lot of designers fall into the trap of testing emails only in their browser or an app like Litmus. The problem with this is that those designers are not actually interacting with a mobile email, which can lead to buttons being placed in awkward locations, forcing users to make long stretches to reach buttons, which is not exactly a friendly experience.

With these considerations in mind, the best practice when it comes to buttons and CTAs is to test both in the browser and on an actual mobile device. It is your job to make sure that everything is easy to see and even easier to tap – from any orientation.

Don't Forget Plain Text

As discussed above, HTML email is actually sent in two parts: (1) the HTML itself and (2) a plain text option. Some email clients or subscribers block HTML content, usually for security reasons, and instead display only the plain-text option. It is therefore extremely important that your plain text email is just as well-designed as its HTML counterpart.

While plain text may seem just that - plain - there is actually a lot you can do with it from a design standpoint.

The first thing you should do is establish some sort of hierarchy. While you cannot use different font sizes, weights, or color (this is plain text, after all), you can use certain characters and techniques to establish a hierarchy within your plain text email.

A common technique is to use repeated characters like plus or equal signs to delimit sections of content. You may encounter plain text emails like this:

```
view this in your browser.
http://rodriguezcommaj.createsend1.com/t/i-e-mykwk-1-h/

=========================================================
A new guide to Modern HTML Email is in the works...
=========================================================

In case you forgot - My name is Jason Rodriguez and I'm writing a new guide to a pain point
for many - HTML email. I really appreciate your interest in the guide and look forward to
sharing it with the design community later this summer.

I'll be sending out updates on the guide as well as some interesting articles and tips over
the coming month or two working up to the guide's release.

Don't worry, I won't drown your inbox. If you ever want to unsubscribe, please do:

http://rodriguezcommaj.createsend1.com/t/i-u-mykwk-1-k/

I promise to work hard and provide as much value as I can to insure that you don't, though.

While I work on Modern HTML Email - why not check out a recent article on the biggest mistake
that you can make in HTML email marketing:

http://rodriguezcommaj.com/blog/HTML-Email-The-Biggest-Mistake

You can also keep up with everything on my blog ** http://rodriguezcommaj.com/blog ** or
follow me on Twitter ** http://twitter.com/rodriguezcommaj **

Until next time,

Jason Rodriguez

=========================================================
You are receiving this email because you showed an interest in one of my projects. Thanks for
that! If you ever get sick of me, just unsubscribe here:

http://rodriguezcommaj.createsend1.com/t/i-u-mykwk-1-u/.

If you liked it, why not forward it to a friend?

http://rodriguezcommaj.forwardtomyfriend.com/i-1-2AD73FFF-mykwk-1-o

http://rodriguezcommaj.createsend1.com/t/i-tw-mykwk-1-m/

Jason Rodriguez - P.O. Box 2031, Royal Oak, MI 48068

Thanks to Campaign Monitor ** http://campaignmonitor.com ** for their generous support and
excellent product! I highly recommend using their service for your next email campaign.

http://campaignmonitor.com/?email
```

You can see how sections are clearly established, allowing for easy and natural reading.

You also need to think about your links. The beauty of HTML email is that you can code hyperlinks into the design, allowing users to click through to wherever you want them to go. Plain text doesn't afford the same luxury. Therefore, you need to clearly display the URLs you want readers to notice.

Most ESPs provide the functionality to automatically generate a plain text email from your HTML email, and, more often than not, they just slap all URLs inline with little regard as to how that impedes both the text and your readers' ability to notice the URLs. I recommend taking the time to either drop URLs down on their own line (as long as it doesn't break the flow of reading) or clearly mark them in your own way, such as in the following example.

```
While I work on Modern HTML Email - why not check out a recent article on the biggest mistake
that you can make in HTML email marketing:

http://rodriguezcommaj.com/blog/HTML-Email-The-Biggest-Mistake

You can also keep up with everything on my blog ** http://rodriguezcommaj.com/blog ** or
follow me on Twitter ** http://twitter.com/rodriguezcommaj **
```

Finally, you can always liven up your plain text emails for readers who actually see them by making them more visually appealing. Plain text has a long and rich history, and it is easy to find examples online of cool plain text documents. One of the most fun ways to spice up a plain text email is to add a little ASCII art. Who wouldn't mind seeing something like this in their inbox?

```
view this in your browser.
http://rodriguezcommaj.createsend1.com/t/i-e-mykwk-1-h/
```

Just make sure your message isn't obscured by your cheekiness.

Now that you have a handle on some of the principles behind designing modern HTML email, let's dive into actually building something.

Email code can often get fiddly and it's relatively easy to lose hours chasing bugs - getting a second opinion, or taking a break for 10 minutes, usually helps get a fresh perspective.

Elliot Ross
Action Rocket

Building
Modern Email

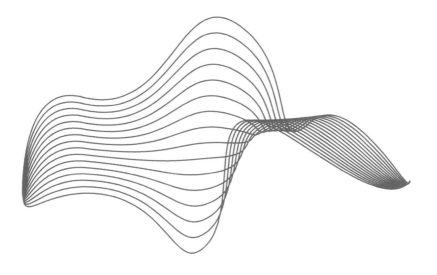

Overview

This section focuses on the techniques needed to actually build an email. Whenever I am learning something new, I like to see how a complete solution is built. I think that it is generally easier to see the whole picture and adapt it as necessary for other situations than to try to piece together a bunch of disparate parts. Thus, in this section, I will show you how to build a complete HTML email. I will go through the process of building an email step by step so you are able to see how things are structured and styled. I have kept my examples pretty general and basic so that what you learn here can easily be adapted for different types of emails.

Starting Out

Every email has a beginning, and that beginning is the **doctype**. There are a few flavors of the HTML **doctype**, including the ever succinct one for HTML5:

```
<!DOCTYPE html>
```

I wish we could keep our code that clean, but for reasons of reliability and compatibility we will be using the XHTML 1.0 Transitional **doctype**:

```
<!DOCTYPE html PUBLIC "-//W3C//DTD XHTML 1.0 Transitional//EN" "http://www.
w3.org/TR/xhtml1/DTD/xhtml1-transitional.dtd">
```

Why choose one **doctype** over another? The main reason is that some email clients can get buggy rendering things like margins and padding with a certain **doctype**. XHTML 1.0 Transitional is your best bet for whipping those clients into shape.

You can sometimes get away with other doctypes, or even no doctype

---

at all, but it is generally a good idea to stick to what is normally regarded as the industry standard.

If you have done any web design, then you should know that the next section of the email is the head. For a long time, email designers in general did not pay much attention to the head. I have seen a lot of legacy emails that do not even include this section. The reason behind this lack of attention is that most web-based email clients strip out the head so that no scripts or styles interfere with the actual rendering of the page, making focusing on the head a waste of time.

However, with the advent of mobile devices and Webkit-based clients, the head of emails has become extraordinarily useful. In fact, it is where most of the responsive magic is implemented.

Before I start implementing any responsive stuff, here is what a basic head setup looks like:

```
<!DOCTYPE html PUBLIC "-//W3C//DTD XHTML 1.0 Transitional//EN" "http://www.
w3.org/TR/xhtml1/DTD/xhtml1-transitional.dtd">
<html xmlns="http://www.w3.org/1999/xhtml">
  <head>
    <meta http-equiv="Content-Type" content="text/html; charset=UTF-8" />
    <meta name="viewport" content="width=device-width, initial-scale=1" />
    <title>Four New Designs at Mnml Pstr</title>
    <style type="text/css">

    /* Take care of image borders and formatting */
      img { max-width:600px !important; outline:none; text-decoration:none; -ms-
interpolation-mode: bicubic; }
      a img { border:none; }
    </style>
  </head>
</html>
```

You may notice a few things here. First, I included a title for the document out of courtesy to anyone that might be viewing it in a browser. Next, there is a weird meta tag that sets the viewport width equal to the device-width, with an initial-scale. This is used for mobile devices so that when the email is viewed on smaller screens it is displayed at the proper scale and the responsive, width-based settings work. Finally, within a `style` tag, I have set some basic properties to make sure the images don't have any borders and are rendered well across clients.

This is a good setup to work from. Later on, I will show you how to write some more specific CSS in the style tag to get the responsive template working.

There are two ways to go about writing your CSS. The first is writing all of your CSS inline. The second is writing your CSS in the head and using a service like Premailer to automatically generate HTML with inline styles.

I tend to prefer the former method when coding emails. While the latter method can be quicker and look cleaner, it can cause you to run into a few problems. For example, if you are relying on complicated cascades or selectors, the inline tool may have problems parsing your email. More importantly, you lose some comprehension of the code if a tool is generating it for you. I like to look at my code and know what is going on immediately. If I write it myself, then I won't have any trouble doing that. However, if I rely on a tool to write my code for me, I am going to waste a lot of valuable time trying to understand it when I need to go back and make a change or an update in the future.

Once you get a feel for what is possible and what should be done within an email, feel free to use your ESP's built-in formatter or a third-party tool like PreMailer to speed up your workflow, but starting out, I recommend keeping nearly everything inline.

Except for the responsive stuff. We'll get to that soon.

Your Old Enemy, Your New Best Friend

For a long time, the web was ruled by tables. If you have worked in the field for more than a few years, you will remember building websites using tables for your entire layout. You probably have fond memories of spacer GIFs too.

In 2003, designer Dave Shea introduced a little site named the *CSS Zen Garden*. Along with books like *Designing With Web Standards* and publications like *A List Apart* (both created by the legendary Jeffrey Zeldman), *CSS Zen Garden* helped establish Cascading Style Sheets as the new standard when styling HTML websites. While some developers stuck with (and still use) tables and inline styles for structure and styling on the web, the advantages of separating presentation from structure are now readily apparent.

Tables have always been a huge pain in the ass. Deep nesting of tables leads to a lot of math, complicated image slicing, and a maintenance nightmare. Tables are tricky to create and even harder to change after they are created. They were our old worst enemy, and rightly so. Now you must learn to make them your new best friend. Because email clients do not support CSS, especially the box model or floats, in any consistent way, tables should be the foundation of ALL of your layouts.

So dust off your table skills and get ready to see what you need to know about using them in email.

As I mentioned above, you should be using tables for all of your layouts. Very few email clients have good support for the box model, so using `divs` and floats is out of the question. You can still use `divs` as a generic container, but I wouldn't recommend using them in a structural way. And don't even think about newer semantic elements in HTML5. Elements like `section` or `article` will have abysmal support. If you know the majority of your subscribers will be using a Webkit-based client, you can test some newer stuff out, but for most situations I would steer clear of anything beyond tables.

Remember when using tables that it is important to always set your table properties inline, requiring you to use some of those attributes you likely have not seen years. Attributes like `cellpadding`, `cellspacing`, `width`, and `height` should always be set inline at the table level. The general rule is that you should always rely on, and always remember to declare, HTML attributes wherever you can. Support across clients, especially older ones, is much better for HTML attributes than for CSS. Later on, I will discuss how to use CSS to override HTML attributes as needed.

Here is an example of a containing table, within which you can build out the rest of your email:

```
<body bgcolor="#efefef" style="background-color:#efefef; -webkit-text-size-
adjust: none;">
  <table align="center" border="0" cellpadding="0" cellspacing="0" width="600"
id="emailContainer" style="display:block; max-width:600px; background-
color:#efefef;">
    <tr>
      <td align="center" valign="top">
        ...Put Content In Here...
      </td>
    </tr>
  </table>
</body>
```

All other tables will be nested within this structure.

Building Content

I have an affinity for simple things, especially when it comes to graphic design. I have always thought about starting up an online poster shop that deals in minimalist posters. Naturally, I would use email marketing to build relationships with customers and drive them to the store. So, for this guide, I will be building out what one of those newsletters might look like.

For the purposes of this guide, I will call the store Mnml Pstr (clever, huh?). My sample newsletter will announce some new additions to the shop and contain some content from the company blog.

Personally, I love keeping emails simple, single-column affairs – especially when I am targeting a mobile audience. But I want to show you how to build something that is more in line with current email marketing practices. Therefore, the Mnml Pstr email will be a mixture of single- and double-column sections with a fair amount of imagery and content.

Let me start by adding some of that content. Most emails contain some pre-message content before anything else in the email. This pre-message content is usually in the form of a preheader that displays in some inboxes, as well as a link to view the email in a browser and a link to unsubscribe. I am going to break a bit with tradition here and drop my "view email" stuff down to the bottom of my email. I want the top of my email to be nice and clean, but I still want to include that stuff somewhere. In my opinion, and for the purposes of my example, the end of the email is an ideal place for it.

Why include a link to view the email in a browser?

Well, because every email campaign is bound to run into display issues in certain clients, it helps to provide an alternate view for subscribers. Because we are building with HTML and CSS, viewing an email in the browser will, in theory (no guarantee for IE), show the email, and your message, in the best light.

It is not absolutely necessary to provide this link, but it is a good practice. Anything you can do to make your subscribers' experience more positive is worth it. And with funky email clients and disabled images, the best practice is to include a link to a browser version in every email you send.

Plus, most ESPs provide some sort of template language that makes implementing this link very easy. So the better question is: why not?

Let's look at the preheader. Notice that it sits outside of the main container table. I do this mainly for separation in my code, so that I can easily find and update the preheader as needed.

```
<body bgcolor="#efefef" style="background-color:#efefef; -webkit-text-size-
adjust: none;">
  <span class="preheader" style="display:none; color:#efefef;">
    Four new posters just arrived in the shop!
  </span>
  <table align="center" border="0" cellpadding="0" cellspacing="0" width="600"
id="emailContainer" style="display:block; max-width:600px; background-
color:#efefef;">
    <tr>
      <td align="center" valign="top">
        ...Put Content In Here...
      </td>
    </tr>
  </table>
</body>
```

You will notice that I have hidden the pre-header message here. This is because I don't want to display that content within the email itself. This is a commonly used trick for email clients that display content from the email in the inbox. I am sure you have all seen a message that looks like this:

Wouldn't it be better if you saw something like this instead?

Using the preheader trick allows you to pull this off. Keep in mind that this trick does not work for every inbox, but for the ones in which it does, you will likely see a nice jump in your open rate. Note that I am using both `display:none` and setting the text to a color that matches the background of the email to hide the preheader. Most email clients will respect the `display:none` rule, but for those that don't (such as

Lotus Notes), making the text the same color as the background will provide a similar result.

Next, before adding any images, you should start blocking in your text content.

I will start with a simple welcome message spanning the full width of the email:

```
<table border="0" cellpadding="0" cellspacing="0" width="100%">
  <tr>
    <td align="center" valign="top">
      <table border="0" cellpadding="10" cellspacing="0" width="100%">
        <tr>
          <td align="center" valign="top">
            <span style="font-family:Arial; font-size:28px; color:#444444;">Mnml
Pstr Adds Four New Designs.</span>
            <br />
            <br />
            <span style="font-family:Arial; font-size:16px; color:#888888;">The
designers at <a href="http://mnmlpstr.com" style="font-family:Arial; font-
size:14px; color:#16A086; text-decoration:none;"><span style="font-family:Arial;
font-size:14px; color:#16A086; text-decoration:none;">MnmlPstr.com</span></
a> have been hard at work on four new designs. Featuring simple shapes and bold
colors, these additions are sure to sell out!</span>
            <br />
            <br />
            <table width="50%" cellspacing="0" cellpadding="0" border="0"
style="background-color:#16A086;">
              <tr>
                <td style="padding: 18px 20px 18px 20px; font-family: Arial,
sans-serif; color: #ffffff; font-size: 18px; text-align: center;">
                  <a href="http://mnmlpstr.com" style="text-decoration: none;
color: #ffffff;">Get Them Now</a>
                </td>
                • • •
```

Mnml Pstr Adds Four New Designs.

The designers at MnmlPstr.com have been hard at work on four new designs.
Featuring simple shapes and bold colors, these additions are sure to sell out!

I am not doing anything too fancy with styling in my sample email in order to keep it simple and make it easy to follow along. You will notice that I am using a `span` for styling rather than elements like `h1`, `p`, etc. I have seen elements like those break down too many times in clients to rely on them. A `span` will allow you to reliably style content without having to worry about weird defaults for other elements throughout clients.

The same reasoning applies for my decision to use line breaks instead of paragraph tags for text separation. Email clients implement paragraphs in a variety of ways, whereas I have found that line breaks work well for adding reliable spacing between sections of text across clients.

Take note of that hyperlink, too. You will see that I am applying styles both to the `href` and a `span` within. While the repetition may bother some, it is necessary for links to display properly across clients. Some clients honor the styles on the `href`, others on the `span`, so you should cover both cases. This helps keep the template and the styling robust across clients.

Another thing you should note is that the message is in its own table with a `width` of 100%. This will help when looking at the email on a mobile device. The table holding the message will always be the full width of the containing table, so when you need to fit the email to a specific width on mobile devices, you simply need to adjust the `width` on that main containing table as opposed to all of the tables within it.

Next I will add a title for our brand. Mnml Pstr keeps things simple, so I won't be using any fancy logos here. Instead, I will just style up some text for our branding:

```
<table border="0" cellpadding="0" cellspacing="0" width="100%">
  <tr>
    <td align="center" valign="top">
      <table border="0" cellpadding="10" cellspacing="0" width="100%">
        <tr>
          <td align="center" valign="top">
            <a href="http://mnmlpstr.com" style="font-family:Arial; font-
size:60px; color:#444444; text-decoration:none;"><span style="font-family:Arial;
font-size:60px; color:#444444; text-decoration:none;">Mnml Pstr</span></a>
          </td>
        </tr>
      </table>
    </td>
  </tr>
</table>
```

This text looks good, is true to the brand, and, more importantly, will show up in every client even when images are disabled.

As I mentioned earlier, I plan to include some content from the Mnml Pstr blog in my sample email. Because this content is going to be in the same single-column style as the copy above, I will mark it up right now.

```html
<table border="0" cellpadding="0" cellspacing="0" width="100%" style="max-
width:600px;">
  <tr>
    <td align="center" valign="top">
      <table border="0" cellpadding="10" cellspacing="0" width="100%">
        <tr>
          <td align="center" valign="top">
            <br />
            <br />
            <span style="font-family:Arial; font-size:28px;
color:#444444;"><b>From Our Blog</b><br />A New Home</span>
            <br />
            <br />
            <div style="text-align:left;">
              <span style="font-family:Arial; font-size:16px;
color:#888888;">We've been growing over here at Mnml Pstr, which is both good and
bad. Working in a shared space has been great, but with the additions of Anne,
Deirdre, and Jack - we've found ourselves in need of a new place to call home.</
span>
              <br />
              <br />
              <span style="font-family:Arial; font-size:16px;
color:#888888;">After a tiring search for the perfect space, we found a stunning
location right off of Main Street. The best part is that we have a real
storefront and have opened up shop with some of our best minimal posters! We're
still unpacking some of our boxes but are thrilled to be able to stretch out and
showcase our work for all who stop by.</span>
              <br />
              <br />
              <span style="font-family:Arial; font-size:16px;
color:#888888;">While there's still some decorating to be done, we snapped some
pictures for you to check out.</span>
            </div>
            <br />
            <br />
            <a href="http://mnmlpstr.com" style="font-family:Arial; font-
size:22px; color:#16A086; text-decoration:none;"><span style="font-family:Arial;
font-size:22px; color:#16A086; text-decoration:none;">Want to see what it looks
like?</span></a>
            <br />
            <br />
            <span style="font-family:Arial; font-size:28px;
color:#E84C3D;">&hearts; &hearts; &hearts;</span>
          </td>
        </tr>
      </table>
    </td>
  </tr>
</table>
```

Mnml Pstr

Mnml Pstr Adds Four New Designs.

The designers at MnmlPstr.com have been hard at work on four new designs.
Featuring simple shapes and bold colors, these additions are sure to sell out!

From Our Blog
A New Home

We've been growing over here at Mnml Pstr, which is both good and bad.
Working in a shared space has been great, but with the additions of Anne,
Deirdre, and Jack - we've found ourselves in need of a new place to call home.

After a tiring search for the perfect space, we found a stunning location right off of
Main Street. The best part is that we have a real storefront and have opened up
shop with some of our best minimal posters! We're still unpacking some of our
boxes but are thrilled to be able to stretch out and showcase our work for all who
stop by.

While there's still some decorating to be done, we snapped some pictures for you
to check out.

Want to see what it looks like?

When marking up this content, I followed the same conventions
as above: a 100%-width table for the content with line breaks for
separation and individual spans for styling. While blog entries may
help build the ever-important subscriber-marketer relationship, they
likely won't drive many people to my hypothetical store. Hopefully
introducing some images and buttons will help take care of this.

In my example, Mnml Pstr is announcing four new posters. I want to

---

display these posters on the desktop in a 2x2 grid with an image for each poster, the poster's title below each image, and a large button for subscribers to press to their hearts' content. I will start with the table structure and titles:

```
<table border="0" cellpadding="0" cellspacing="0" width="600"
class="columnContainer">
  <tr>
    <td align="center" valign="top" width="50%" class="columnSingle">
      <table border="0" cellpadding="10" cellspacing="0" width="100%">
        <tr>
          <td align="center" valign="top" class="columnContent">
            <span style="font-family:Arial; font-size:22px; color:#2A80B9;">Blue
Whale Poster</span>
          </td>
        </tr>
      </table>
    </td>
    <td align="center" valign="top" width="50%" class="columnSingle">
      <table border="0" cellpadding="10" cellspacing="0" width="100%">
        <tr>
          <td align="center" valign="top" class="columnContent">
            <span style="font-family:Arial; font-size:22px; color:#8F44AD;">Plum
Poster</span>
          </td>
        </tr>
      </table>
    </td>
  </tr>
</table>
```

Mnml Pstr

Mnml Pstr Adds Four New Designs.

The designers at MnmlPstr.com have been hard at work on four new designs. Featuring simple shapes and bold colors, these additions are sure to sell out!

Blue Whale Poster   Plum Poster

Clementine Poster   Malbec Poster

You may notice that I have not added the actual images yet, but, fear not, I will get to them soon. First, I want some nice, big, touchable buttons to draw people into the store so they can buy those posters. While I could use images for these buttons (and many people do), I know that a ton of email clients will not display these images by default. I want to avoid causing any confusion for my subscribers, so I am going to make these buttons entirely out of HTML and CSS instead of using images. It may seem a little weird and verbose to use a full table for email buttons, but the support and consistency across email clients provided by this method is fantastic, so bear with me.

```
. . .
<br />
<br />
<table width="100%" cellspacing="0" cellpadding="0" border="0" style="background-
color:#2A80B9;" class="mobileButton">
  <tr>
    <td style="padding: 18px 20px 18px 20px; font-family: Arial, sans-serif;
color: #ffffff; font-size: 18px; text-align: center;">
<a href="http://mnmlpstr.com" style="text-decoration: none; color: #ffffff;">Get
This Poster</a>
    </td>
  </tr>
</table>
. . .
```

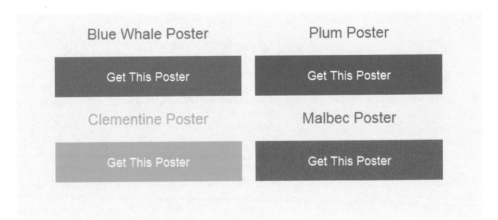

Already the email is looking much better and, more importantly, very clickable. If you want to get a little fancier with your buttons, you could go the image route, but be prepared for the reality that, by default, most clients will not display buttons made from images.

Another great option for buttons was introduced not long ago by Campaign Monitor developer Stig Morten Myre. His solution is Bulletproof Buttons, which allows you to style your buttons to your liking using CSS3 and background images. This option maintains consistency in Microsoft clients by taking advantage of their VML code for styling – something that no mortal would have attempted before Bulletproof Buttons came along. Even in some of the worst clients, buttons created using Bulletproof Buttons degrade very gracefully so that no user is left out in the cold. Even with VML, the code is not too bad:

```
<div><!--[if mso]>
  <v:roundrect xmlns:v="urn:schemas-microsoft-com:vml" xmlns:w="urn:schemas-
microsoft-com:office:word" href="http://emailbtn.net/" style="height:44px;v-text-
anchor:middle;width:200px;" arcsize="0%" stroke="f" fill="t">
    <v:fill type="tile" src=""http://i.imgur.com/nft2g.gif"" color="#466897" />
    <w:anchorlock/>
    <center style="color:#ffffff;font-family:sans-serif;font-size:13px;font-
weight:bold;">Bulletproof Buttons</center>
  </v:roundrect>
<![endif]--><![if !mso]><a href="http://emailbtn.net/"
style="background-color:#466897;background-image:url("http://i.imgur.com/nft2g.
gif");border-radius:px;color:#ffffff;display:inline-block;font-family:sans-
serif;font-size:13px;font-weight:bold;line-height:44px;text-align:center;text-
decoration:none;width:200px;-webkit-text-size-adjust:none;">Bulletproof Buttons</
a><![endif]>
</div>
```

The above code outputs this button:

For now, I'm going to stick to table-based HTML buttons. However, I encourage you to play around with other techniques — as long as you promise to test your implementation.

The final section in any email is the footer, which should always contain a few things. You may recall that the CAN-SPAM Act dictates that certain information and links must be included in commercial emails. The footer is where I will be placing that information, along with anything else needed in the email that isn't core to my message.

My footer will contain the following: (1) a brief message about why my subscribers are receiving the email (note that this information is not necessary, but recommended as a courtesy to subscribers) (2) a link to unsubscribe from the email list, and (3) my physical mailing address for compliance with the CAN-SPAM Act. A lot of companies also use the footer for disclaimers or additional legal information — if these things are necessary to your email, the footer is the place for them. The footer in my example ends up containing a sizeable chunk of code, as seen on the following page.

I will bump down the text-size a bit because all of the information contained in the footer is secondary to the main content above. However, you should note that I made sure the unsubscribe link is prominent. Though it sucks losing subscribers, not providing an easy way for subscribers to opt-out of your list is a terrible practice and should be avoided.

```
<table border="0" cellpadding="0" cellspacing="0" width="100%" style="max-
width:600px;">
  <tr>
    <td align="center" valign="top">
      <table border="0" cellpadding="10" cellspacing="0" width="100%">
        <tr>
          <td align="left" valign="top">
            <span style="font-family:Arial; font-size:14px;
color:#888888;">You're getting this email because you love our products over
at <a href="http://mnmlpstr.com" style="font-family:Arial; font-size:14px;
color:#16A086; text-decoration:none;"><span style="font-family:Arial; font-
size:14px; color:#16A086; text-decoration:none;">MnmlPstr.com</span></a> - We
really appreciate all of your interest and look forward to delighting you for
years to come. If you ever get sick of us, please <a href="http://mnmlpstr.com/
unsubscribe" style="font-family:Arial; font-size:14px; color:#16A086; text-
decoration:none;"><span style="font-family:Arial; font-size:14px; color:#16A086;
text-decoration:none;">unsubscribe from our list</span></a>.</span>
            <br />
            <br />
            <span style="font-family:Arial; font-size:14px; color:#888888;">If
this email looks weird, <a href="http://mnmlpstr.com/email" style="font-
family:Arial; font-size:14px; color:#16A086; text-decoration:none;"><span
style="font-family:Arial; font-size:14px; color:#16A086; text-
decoration:none;">check it out online</span></a>.</span>
            <br />
            <br />
            <span class="applefix" style="font-family:Arial; font-size:14px;
color:#888888;">
              <b>Our Digs:</b><br />
              Mnml Pstr<br />
              123 Second Street<br />
              Anywhere Town, USA 45678
            </span>
            <br />
            <br />
          </td>
        </tr>
      </table>
    </td>
  </tr>
</table>
```

Here is how our full email is looking, albeit a bit zoomed out:

Not too bad. There is a strong structural base and some solid type. However, it probably looks like it is missing something – imagery. A good promotional email should include some imagery to delight and entice subscribers. How to best implement images will be the focus of the next section, aptly titled . . .

Images

Images (along with clickable links) are the main reason that people favor HTML emails over plain-text emails for marketing. They can make or break a campaign, so it's important to get them right. If you come from a web design background, you may think that you have images in HTML figured out, but I would wager that if you try applying some of your usual web design techniques to placing images in an HTML email, you will be pulling your hair out in no time.

This section focuses on how to use images properly in HTML email (so you can keep your hair intact).

Using my newsletter email example, the first thing I want to do is add a large hero image at the top of the email. This is common practice in emails, and a good place to start.

If you have a web design background, you might try doing something like this:

```
<img src="/hero.jpg" />
```

But try that in an email and you're screwed. Because emails are not going to be associated with any directory structure, you always need to use an absolute path for your images. It is essential that you host your images on a reliable, public-accessible server. Most ESPs do this for you.

Here is a better way to add your hero image:

```
<img src="http://assets.modernhtmlemail.com/hero.jpg" />
```

Two issues you will likely run into when coding your images are

---

the sizing of your images and the padding (or margins) around your images. You can avoid sizing issues by declaring your image dimensions via HTML attributes. You can avoid spacing issues by adding a `display:block` rule.

Here is a much more robust image tag:

```
<img src="http://assets.modernhtmlemail.com/hero.jpg" width="580px"
height="290px" border="0" alt="1 2 3 4" style="display:block;" />
```

That looks pretty good.

Next, I will do the same thing for those new posters that are featured in the body of the email. Following the same rules, I will simply add them to our template:

```
. . .
<tr>
  <td class="columnContent">
    <img src="http://assets.modernhtmlemail.com/posterblue.jpg" width="280"
height="420" border="0"  alt="Blue Whale" style="display:block;"
class="columnImage" />
  </td>
</tr>
. . .
```

Here is a look at a row of posters:

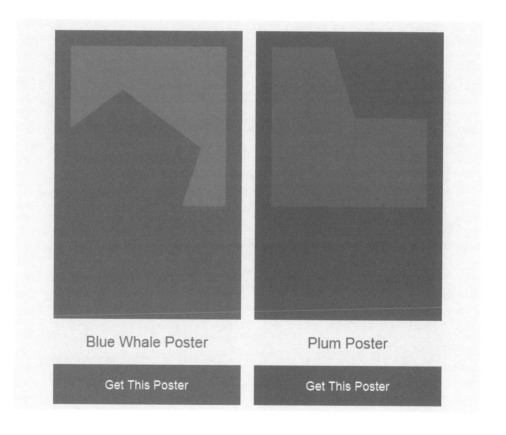

Not too shabby. My images are in place, and I might think about calling it a day here. But if you have been following along, you will know that nearly every email client will block my images by default.

Here is what my subscribers will most likely see if I leave my email as it is coded so far:

That is certainly a problem. What can I do about it?

The best way to tackle image blocking is by utilizing the image's `alt` attribute. Using the `alt` attribute, you can provide the reader with information even when images are blocked by default. What's more, you can style your `alt` attribute so that the email still looks pretty damned good when images are blocked.

Thus, the solution to the image-blocking problem is to simply provide good, descriptive copy in the `alt` attribute and define the styles within the image tag. Here is how I would do that for the example newsletter:

```
<img src="http://assets.modernhtmlemail.com/posterblue.jpg" width="280"
height="420" border="0"  alt="Blue Whale" style="display:block; max-width:280px;
color:#efefef; text-align:center; font-family:Arial; font-size:28px; font-
weight:bold; background-color:#2A80B9;" class="columnImage" />
```

Now, even if images are disabled, most email clients will display something that still looks great:

You can go to town with styling blocked images. If you search around online, you can find some creative campaigns that delight and surprise when their images are blocked. The thing to keep in mind is that even a small amount of information about your images is far better than not accounting for image-blocking at all.

At this point, the sample email is looking pretty good. It has a solid, table-based structure to build on, some good inline styles for content, and a robust image solution. But this guide is all about modern HTML email, so you may be asking yourself, "Where does this responsive stuff kick in?" I will dig into that next.

Responsive Strategies

With mobile email opens on the rise and some statistics already having them outweighing desktop opens, it is extremely important to make your email campaigns as mobile-friendly as possible.

While it may not be possible to use some of the following techniques in all emails, a typical email can either use them outright or riff on them as needed to provide subscribers with the best possible experience on a range of devices.

In his seminal 2011 work, *Responsive Web Design*, designer Ethan Marcotte established the tenets of the responsive web. One of those tenets is a flexible grid. In web design, pages are built on top of some sort of grid, which is a structure - as simple or as complex as needed - that places the elements on the page. Traditionally, these grids were fixed. They used static units (pixels) for their sizing.

Marcotte established that one of the most important parts of designing responsively was to make these fixed grids flexible by using relative units to describe their size - units like percentages or ems. These units, along with adjusting the display properties of elements via media queries, allow the grid to flow and adapt to the device size, effectively decoupling the design from the device and making web pages more flexible and future-proof.

Responsive emails work the same way. Although email designers have a more limited set of techniques available to them than web designers due to inconsistent email clients, it is still possible to use a flexible layout to adapt emails for viewing on different devices.

For example, you will notice that, apart from two container tables, all of the tables in my sample email have percentage-based widths. This allows for those tables to flow and fill their containers. On the desktop, both container tables are 600px wide. However, when the email is viewed on a mobile device, they will become fluid and adapt to the screen of that device.

Why 600 pixels wide?

Most email clients initially display emails in a preview pane. Nearly all of these preview panes are very limited when it comes to screen real estate.

If you make your emails too wide, the content that extends beyond that small preview pane will not be visible. Therefore, current practices dictate that you should keep your emails around 600 pixels wide. With larger screens becoming more common in recent years, you may be able to get away with making them wider - even upwards of 800 pixels - but I recommend playing it safe and keeping your emails between 500 - 650 pixels wide.

Up in the **head** of my email, I am going to introduce a CSS3 media query. Media queries allow you to target specific devices by looking for things like screen size or pixel density and feeding different styles to devices that fit those targets. They are easy enough to read:

```
@media only screen and (max-width:600px) {
    ... INSERT CSS RULES HERE ...
}
```

Within those parentheses, you can use a number of rules to target devices. For our purposes, I am not worried about hitting anything too specific. It should be good enough to target anything below 600 pixels wide for my mobile styles. Thus, I will simply use 600px as my **max-width** with the result that whenever a screen is narrower than 600px my mobile styles will override my default styling.

Next, to get my container tables to be flexible, I will target the ID and Class and adjust a few properties:

```
@media only screen and (max-width:600px) {
    table[id="emailContainer"] { width:100% !important; }
    table[class="columnContainer"] { width:100% !important; }
}
```

As I add responsive styles, you may notice that I make liberal use of the **!important** declaration. This is just a failsafe to make sure that anything I am doing up here overrides the inline styles in my HTML. Now my container tables are filling the entire mobile display, and any nested tables that are 100% wide will do the same. This obtains the desired result: when the screen-size shrinks, my email shrinks right along with it.

But what about the two-column poster section? If I keep their widths set to 50%, the images, text, and buttons will be difficult to see, read, and use on smaller screens. By using the same technique as in my container tables, I can make them fill the full width of the email. Note that I gave them a class of `columnSingle`. I am going use this to target my CSS:

```
@media only screen and (max-width:600px) {
   table[id="emailContainer"] { width:100% !important; }
   table[class="columnContainer"] { width:100% !important; }
   td[class="columnSingle"] { display:block !important; width:100% !important; }
}
```

With just those two fixes in my media queries, I have a pretty good mobile implementation. But, if you were to look at the email now, you would see that my images are not flowing very well. How do I get my images, fixed to a specific size within my HTML, to be flexible just like my tables?

Easy. Just like this:

```
@media only screen and (max-width:600px) {
   img { width:100% !important; height:auto !important; }
   img[class="columnImage"] { height:auto !important; max-width:480px !important;
width:100% !important; }
   table[id="emailContainer"] { width:100% !important; }
   table[class="columnContainer"] { width:100% !important; }
   td[class="columnSingle"] { display:block !important; width:100% !important; }
}
```

Now, even though we have hard-coded the image sizes using HTML attributes, our flexible solution will override those attributes on devices that support media queries, allowing our images to flow along with the rest of the layout.

I am picky and I know I won't like how the buttons are the full width of the containing table. I think it would be better to make them a bit narrower on smaller screens. Not only would it look nicer, but I think it would also really help to break up that poster section a bit. If you look back at our button code, you will notice that I gave our buttons a class of mobileButton:

```
• • •
<br />
<br />
<table width="100%" cellspacing="0" cellpadding="0" border="0" style="background-
color:#2A80B9;" class="mobileButton">
  <tr>
    <td style="padding: 18px 20px 18px 20px; font-family: Arial, sans-serif;
color: #ffffff; font-size: 18px; text-align: center;">
<a href="http://mnmlpstr.com" style="text-decoration: none; color: #ffffff;">Get
This Poster</a>
    </td>
  </tr>
</table>
• • •
```

Now, in my CSS, I will use that to target my buttons and set the `width`:

```
@media only screen and (max-width:600px) {
  img { width:100% !important; height:auto !important; }
  img[class="columnImage"] { height:auto !important; max-width:480px !important;
width:100% !important; }
  table[id="emailContainer"] { width:100% !important; }
  table[class="columnContainer"] { width:100% !important; }
  table[class="mobileButton"] { width:60% !important; }
  td[class="columnSingle"] { display:block !important; width:100% !important; }
}
```

Now, my buttons feel a bit more like buttons and are still plenty big enough for readers to press.

You could always take things a bit further with your responsive design. For example, you could implement a responsive navigation pattern for website links or adjust the text size for mobile devices. But, for now, I am pretty happy with how my newsletter is looking. I have an email that will display nicely on larger screens for people viewing it on a desktop, and, more importantly, I have an email that adapts itself to devices with smaller screens.

My sample email should serve as an example for how to create robust, responsive emails of your own without too much difficulty. It is clear to see how using the simple techniques discussed in this guide - flexible tables, flexible images, and mobile-targeting with media queries - can give your email campaigns a competitive edge.

Though I am not going to dive too deeply into other responsive techniques in this guide, I want to make you aware of some techniques that are in varying stages of use and acceptance, as well as clue you in to some problems that you are likely to run into when working on responsive emails.

Take a look at the next two pages to see the full email layout for both desktop and mobile views.

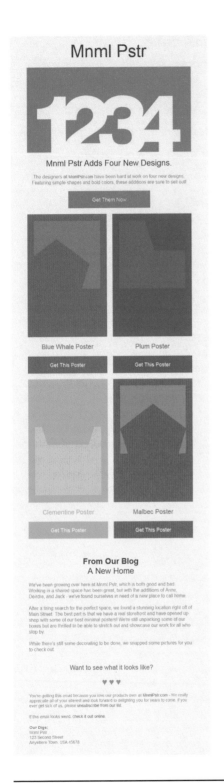

The Desktop Email

This is the desktop view of the Mnml Pstr email.

It is fairly typical of what a lot of email marketing campaigns send to subscribers, with a good mix of images, copy, and calls to action.

It uses a hybrid multi- and single-column approach. If not optimized for mobile devices, the email would be zoomed out - causing the copy to be hard to read and CTAs hard to press.

This leads to a poor user experience for subscribers, which in turn can lead to low conversion rates and unsubscribes.

The Responsive Email

Here is the responsive layout that is seen when viewing the email on a mobile device.

It is the same code as the desktop version, but using fluid containers, fluid images, and CSS3 media queries, it allows the design to adapt and reflow on a mobile device.

Responsive, mobile-friendly emails give subscribers a much better user experience.

Everyone is up in arms about whether or not responsive email design actually performs better. I'm not convinced that we're looking at the right metrics to determine the importance or impact of responsive email design. Most marketers are looking for increases in opens, clicks, conversions, whereas the real improvements are likely in the user experience -- which is much harder to measure. A frustrated or unhappy user is probably much less likely to buy, or open emails in the future.

Justine Jordan
Litmus

Advanced Techniques and Problems

So far this guide has provided a solid base of knowledge and basic techniques from which you should be able to build robust, responsive emails. However, some people might want to explore more advanced techniques to further optimize their emails. In this section, I will discuss the three advanced techniques you are most likely to come across.

With the launch of the iPhone 4, Apple introduced the mass market to what it referred to as a *retina display*. Retina displays essentially have very small pixels at very high densities which allow for crisp images with superb detail. These high-DPI displays make a lot of elements on the web (and in our emails) look brilliant - namely text. However, images that are not optimized for a high-DPI display tend to look uncomfortably blurry on retina displays.

How can you remedy this within your emails?

The solution is fairly simple: produce images that are optimized for the higher-DPI display and scale them down in code to fit your design. The most commonly used scaling technique is saving the images at twice the size of their intended display. For example, I could create the Mnml Pstr hero image, which is coded to be 580x290, at a size of 1160x580 pixels. Then, in my HTML, I could use attributes to set the smaller `width` and `height` - keeping the image's proportions.

When viewed on a high-DPI display, the image will appear very crisp. However, this technique is not without drawbacks. There are two major issues you should consider when using this approach.

First, some email clients do not acknowledge the `width` set on images.

In these clients, the larger images will display at their full size blowing out your entire design and resulting in a broken, hard-to-view email. Lotus Notes and some versions of Outlook are among the clients with this problem. If your subscriber list has a significant portion of users opening in these clients, it is probably best to stick to smaller images so your design will deliver intact. However, if you know that a large portion of your subscribers are using modern email clients or mobile devices to view their emails, you should be safe using this approach - as long as you are comfortable ignoring the next problem.

The second issue is that downloading data on a mobile device can get expensive. By using larger, optimized images you are asking your subscribers to eat into their expensive data plans. Some subscribers may not be keen to do this, and your attempt to optimize your subscribers' viewing experience could result in fewer opens or a high number of unsubscribes.

It is up to you to decide whether your subscribers will really care about optimized images based on what you know about them. If you know that a majority of your subscribers will be viewing your emails on high-DPI displays and will not care about the data cost, then optimize away. However, if you know that your subscriber list is made up of people using a wide variety of email clients, especially if many of your subscribers are using older clients, you should probably stick with the traditional image route. It is likely that many people will not even notice the slight blur of non-optimized images, but as a designer, I know it can be annoying. Because I strive to create robust emails that display well across clients, I generally opt for smaller images at specific sizes, despite the slight blur on high-DPI screens. The designer in me twitches a bit, but the marketer in me knows that the wider support is more important than a perfectly crisp image.

The second advanced technique I want to touch on is the use of `display:none`.

This practice is widely used among responsive designers. While there is an ongoing debate in the web design community about whether or not it is a good practice, most modern CSS frameworks, such as Twitter Bootstrap and Foundation by Zurb, rely on it for a number of tasks. I am sure you can tell by its name what the property does. The use of `display:none` hides the element on which it is set from rendering on a page. This is a wildly useful technique when optimizing an email for mobile viewing. When coupled with media queries, it allows you to clean up your layout and further hone your content for mobile readers.

However, as with most optimization techniques, it has its drawbacks. One drawback is that even though you are hiding content, the hidden content is still downloaded. As with high-DPI images, this can potentially become expensive for your mobile subscribers, and should be considered when deciding whether and when to use this technique. Another issue with using display:none is legacy compatibility. You should know by now that some clients (most notably Lotus Notes and some versions of Outlook) do not play well with certain techniques - `display:none` is one such technique. The result is that whatever you think you are hiding by using `display:none` will still be shown in those clients that do not support it. Thus, if you rely on this technique too heavily, you may end up with emails that look very funky in older clients.

The final advanced technique I will discuss is the use of background images in emails. Background images should be familiar to most web designers. They can be incredibly useful in email designs, albeit with drawbacks similar to those that accompany high-DPI images and hiding content.

Background images will, as you may suspect, add to the amount of data a user needs to download. As with high-DPI images and the use of display:none, this may become expensive for mobile users and should be considered before proceeding with background images.

An issue of greater concern is support. While most mobile devices have great support for background images and cool properties like `background-size:cover`, a lot of older email clients do not have any support for background images. In fact, many clients will not display your background images at all, which is something you need to account for if you are using background images. The best way to do so is by setting a `background-color` that works with your design as a fallback for missing background images. Most clients do support background colors, so you will be covered if you follow this practice.

Despite these issues, there are some pretty cool things you can do with background images. One of my favorites is swapping out images with background images on mobile devices. A big problem with simply scaling images with the screen size, like I did in my sample newsletter, is that if you have any text or complexity in the image, it tends to get lost as the image shrinks. To remedy this, you can hide the image using `display:none` and then substitute a beautifully cropped and designed image via a background image using CSS. This allows you to easily swap out images on mobile and further refine your content to a level not usually seen in email design. I recommend looking into this technique and testing it out in your campaigns. If you can make it work, it is an excellent opportunity to impress your audience.

Though I will not delve into them here (but perhaps in a later guide or blog post), some other responsive techniques I recommend looking into are progressive disclosure, utilizing navigation patterns, and things like animated gifs and videos in email.

Now, on to some of the problems you are likely to encounter. As discussed throughout this book, a major problem for email designers is the lack of continuity of support for email design techniques across email clients. Among the most troublesome email clients and platforms for email designers are Gmail on Android, Outlook.com on Android, Blackberry, and Windows Phone. All of these clients and platforms have shoddy support for CSS and for many of the techniques described within this book. Fortunately, none of these clients or platforms has widespread adoption. However, if you know that a large portion of your subscribers will be viewing your emails on these clients or platforms, you should carefully consider your design choices and attempt to figure out a way to optimize your emails for these clients and platforms.

Of the troublesome clients and platforms listed above, the main one you should consider is Gmail for Android because it has the biggest market share. Gmail for Android has wretched support for CSS, and, unlike the iPhone which will scale an email to fit the screen, it forces users to scroll horizontally to see much of an email's content. STYLECampaign's Anna Yeaman refers to this left-hand column display as the "Grid of Grim" – and rightly so.

When designing for Gmail on Android, it is imperative that you consider your content and keep your important messaging and CTAs visible in the "Grid of Grim."

The results in the other clients and platforms listed above are usually just as bad as the results in Gmail on Android. As always - and as I will discuss further in the next section - I highly recommend that you thoroughly test whatever you design and code before sending it out to your subscribers.

Gmail on Android showing the Grid of Grim.

If you keep all of this stuff in mind (a daunting task, to be sure), you should be pretty well off. There is no such thing as a perfect email, and there is no one right way to create an email. I suggest experimenting with many different techniques to see what works best for you and your campaigns.

Email gives both the designer and the marketer immediate feedback and endless opportunities to optimize. Big and small changes can make a big impact and give teams more ways to collaborate and improve performance.

Compared to other digital marketing channels, it is relatively easy to see the impact of email on business (sometimes even the bottom line). As a designer, it's a way to connect directly to your audience and directly impact them in a way that you can't in other channels.

Justine Jordan
Litmus

Optimizing for Effectiveness

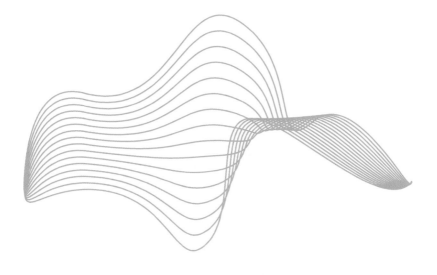

Overview

Designing and building an HTML email is one thing. Designing and building an HTML email that is effective is another. There are three areas in which the effectiveness of your emails is key.

First, you want your emails to be effective across email clients. This means you need a robust template that displays well in a variety of clients. Hopefully this book has given you the tools and information you need build such a template.

Next, you want your emails to be effective at the inbox level. This means that your emails are getting where they need to go and being opened. You can track your inbox-level effectiveness by monitoring your campaign metrics and optimizing your subject lines and sending times.

Finally, you want your emails to be effective from campaign to campaign. This means that you have a subscriber list made up of people who care about your content and take the actions you want them to take when reading your emails.

There are a variety of techniques for improving the effectiveness of your email in these areas. The key techniques are discussed below.

Testing and More Testing

If you read this book and take only one thing away from it, I want it to be this: test the hell out of your emails. You can experiment all you want with different design and optimization techniques, but if your emails do not render well in actual clients, your effort and creativity will not matter.

A couple of the biggest disservices you can do yourself as an email designer are to only design your emails in the browser and to only check your emails in a limited range of inboxes. The key to good email design (or any digital design) is testing. Only by testing in a wide variety of actual clients, or using a service that does this for you, will you learn where your weaknesses lie. Once you recognize where your problems with your emails, you can research the best solutions for fixing them

A small sample of STYLECampaign's devices for testing emails.

So, why not make as many email accounts as possible on as many devices and platforms as you can? You may think I am joking, but having numerous email accounts on multiple devices and platforms is extremely useful for testing your emails. I highly recommend making accounts for as many email clients as you can. And, while it can get expensive, I also recommend getting your hands on as many devices as possible. By testing on actual devices, you can get the feel of how your design works for mobile much better than by scrolling around on your desktop. On actual devices you can get a better idea of how buttons display, how content scrolls, and what breaks down under your thumbs. One way to get your hands on devices is to ask people to donate their old devices for testing purposes. I have found that when friends or family members upgrade their phones, they are happy to hand me their old ones.

I realize that signing up for two dozen email clients and setting up just as many devices (not to mention finding a place to organize and power them) can be time-consuming, tiring, and expensive.

Fortunately, that is not the only option for testing your emails. Another option is to use an email testing service. There are a few services out there that make email testing a breeze at a variety of price points.

The two main players in the email testing field are Litmus and Email on Acid. These services offer similar features. Both allow you to upload your HTML or send your email to a unique email address where it is processed by all of the major and minor email clients. Once the service has finished chewing through your email, it allows you to view screenshots of your campaign in each client, which quickly reveals where your design falls short.

I personally prefer using Litmus for email testing. While it is generally a bit pricier than Email on Acid, the service is absolutely superb. Litmus provides fast results and excellent insight into your email designs. One of my favorite features is its Interactive Testing, which allows you to adjust code on the fly in troublesome clients, making for some pretty quick fixes.

Some ESPs also have testing facilities built into their admin consoles. If you use Campaign Monitor (which you should - it is fantastic), you will find that it allows you to generate tests for any email campaign at a reasonable price. In addition to testing in Litmus, I occasionally run my campaign through Campaign Monitor's testing tool before an important send to make sure that I didn't screw something up along the way.

No matter how you do it – building your own device lab or utilizing a third-party tool for generating previews – testing your emails is an important step in optimizing your emails to be as effective as possible.

Tracking and Metrics

One of the best ways to increase the effectiveness of your campaigns is to track what people are actually doing with your emails and respond accordingly.

Tracking and analyzing campaign metrics helps you understand both the lifecycle of your email and the health of your subscriber list. With these insights, you can hone your design and messaging for the best possible results.

Campaign Monitor provides advanced campaign tracking tools.

Most ESPs make it ridiculously easy to track and view campaign metrics. If you are not taking advantage of their services and reviewing your reports regularly, you are doing something wrong. If you are not using an ESP, I recommend getting with your developers or IT department to figure out a tracking solution.

Once you start getting data and generating reports, it is time to analyze. The following few metrics tend to get the most attention in campaign reports:

Opens tell just that – how many subscribers actually opened your email (with the caveat below). This helps you see if your email is effective at the inbox level. Did your email actually make it to the inbox? Is your subject line good enough to warrant a peek? Keep an eye on this metric, but don't live your life by it because here is the caveat: most tracking relies on subscribers downloading an image, and, because not all subscribers do so, opens are not necessarily the most reliable metric.

Clicks show how many people have actually interacted with your email. If you are tracking things correctly, you can tell which CTAs work best for your subscribers and design future campaigns around similar CTAs.

The **Delivery Rate**, **Bounce Rate**, and **Unsubscribe Rate** are all important metrics to watch. The delivery and bounce rates help you gauge the health of your subscriber list. Sudden changes in either of these rates clue you into critical situations, such as your emails being marked as spam or being put on a blacklist. The unsubscribe rate lets you know when you are losing relevancy with subscribers. If your unsubscribe rate jumps, you may need to reassess your campaign strategy.

The **Conversion Rate**, if you are set up to track it, is one of the most important indicators of a campaign's success. By utilizing campaign-specific links, it tracks users on your sites after they click through a link. This allows you to see how many people perform certain actions on your site after coming from one of your email campaigns (your conversion rate). A high conversion rate is a magical thing. If you are good enough to have one, keep doing what you are doing - it is working.

There are a number of other metrics that vary in importance based on what kinds of campaigns you are sending. The main thing to remember is that you need to look at and understand your campaign reporting. Second to obtaining direct feedback from subscribers, analyzing your metrics is the best way to gain insights into your campaign strategy and optimize your future emails accordingly.

Split Testing and List Segmentation

The final optimization methods I want to discuss are split testing and list segmentation. If you have done any kind of marketing, both concepts should be familiar to you. For those of you who are not familiar with these concepts, I will go over them briefly.

Split testing consists of having two or more variations of an email and sending each variation to an equal number of subscribers. Metrics are collected for each version and compared to see which design performs best. The best-performing design is then used for a larger send or as the basis for future designs.

Split testing is an excellent way to gain insight into how different types of content work within your campaigns. Many people seem intimidated by split testing or think it takes a lot of work to set up. In reality, it is one of the easier methods for optimizing your email campaigns and honing in on what does and does not work for you and your subscribers. It is far easier and quicker to compare an A/B split than to compare changes in creative between full campaigns. It is usually more fun, too. I like to think of split testing as riffing on a theme - playing jazz with emails. If you are working in a team, feel free to place bets on the winner to make things more interesting.

Common splits test things like copy, wording and placement of calls to action, imagery, and subject lines. Subject lines are a major factor in the success of your campaigns, and it is very important to take your time coming up with them and testing their effectiveness. Split testing is a great way to do this.

Subject lines are how you make your first impression on subscribers. Therefore, it is important to make an impact if you want your emails opened. The most important thing is to ensure that your subject lines are highly relevant to your audience and clearly state what is in the email.

A good rule of thumb is to keep your subject lines as succinct as possible – shorter is always better, so long as your message gets across. Numerous studies (check the references in the back of this guide) have been done on the ideal subject line length. There is no consensus as to that magic character count, but most studies have shown subject lines with a character count of 28-39 to be most effective. It's increasingly important to keep your subject line length in mind when writing for the mobile inbox, as email clients on mobile devices truncate subject lines at varying character counts. If your subject line is too long, chances are good that it will be cut off when viewed on a mobile device.

Just like with the content of your emails, you do not want your subject line to come across as spam. MailChimp has done studies that have shown three key phrases that usually contribute to this perception: Help, Percent Off, and Reminder. I would also add using things like ALL CAPS and lots of exclamation points!!!

I also recommend experimenting with personalization, localization, and other techniques such as phrasing your subject line as a question, using a sense of urgency, or even adding in special characters or symbols. Anything you can do to set yourself apart in the inbox is beneficial, just keep it relevant to your audience and the content of your email.

For links to more information on subject lines, check the reference section in the back of the book.

List segmentation is fairly self-explanatory. It involves breaking up your subscriber list into groups based on certain information and sending different email creative tailored to each group.

You may be thinking, "isn't that the same as split testing?" It is close, but in split testing you are running a test based on different versions of an email without considering the preferences of the subscribers in your test groups, whereas in list segmentation, you are sending different versions of an email based on the preferences of your subscribers and the groups in which you have placed them. This allows you to send emails that have a better chance of capturing your subscribers' interest than if you sent the same email to all of your subscribers.

List segmentation hinges on the assumption that you have some known data about your subscribers that allows you to place them in different groups. Some ideas for grouping are by your subscribers' ages, by products they have purchased from you, or by a specific data point that was collected on your site. However you decide to group your subscribers, the idea is that the subscribers in each segmented group have either expressed a common interest or share some demographic characteristic.

The goal of list segmentation is to tailor your emails to the interests of each group. For example, if you run an ecommerce site that sells sporting goods, you could collect subscribers on various pages throughout your site and then segment your list based on the page on which the subscriber signed up. This will separate your subscribers who are interested in shoes from those who are interested in cycling from those who are interested in water sports, etc. You can then target those segmented groups with content that is relevant to their interests rather than attempting to capture the interest of all your subscribers with one general email.

Remaining relevant to subscribers is a paramount concern of email marketers. The more the content of an email speaks to the specific interests of a subscriber, the better the marketer-subscriber relationship will be. As discussed early on in this book, one of the main purposes of email marketing is to develop a strong marketer-subscriber relationship. Split testing and list segmentation help email marketers to maintain a healthy subscriber-marketer relationship and to achieve and maintain relevancy with their subscribers.

Optimizing your emails is an ongoing process. It is something that should be integrated into the design of your emails from the outset and should be considered continually as your design progresses. From your initial design to testing to metrics and back to adjusting your design, everything is connected and important.

In its most boiled down state, here is my advice for success in email marketing: never stop working to make your campaigns better, monitor and understand your metrics, and stay relevant to your audience.

The most important part of any email campaign is to take everything you read on blogs, forums, etc. with a pinch of salt.

These studies, stats, and infographics are informative and can be helpful but you need to test what works for you.

Alex Ilhan
eMosaic

Next Steps

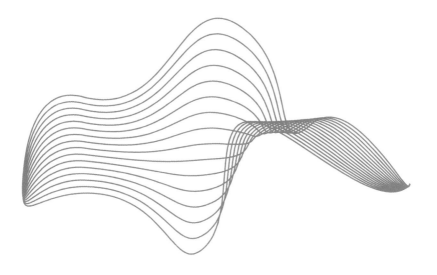

As I bring this book to a close, I would like to leave you with a few thoughts.

Though email has been around for a long, long time, the state of email is far behind that of the web itself. Due to a wide variety of email clients and an even wider range of support for markup and styles, HTML email has traditionally been a drab affair. Because the techniques for building emails have long been stuck in the past, most email campaign designs have been stuck there as well. What's worse is that, because of the challenges involved and the techniques used in email design, most web designers look down on HTML email and hardly consider it an endeavor worth their creative energy.

Fortunately, recent years have seen a renaissance in both HTML email design and coding practices. The mobile revolution has led to the application of responsive techniques, such as those outlined in this book. More and more companies have recognized the value in email marketing and have increased their efforts in the field. Big name brands and small agencies alike are pushing designs forward, modernizing email as we know it. And while email designers still have to contend with the challenges of technological limitations and a myriad of different email clients, the email field has brightened in the past few years.

A lot of clever and talented people have been working hard to make email design. They have also been working to make the email marketing industry more of a community by sharing best practices, openly critiquing each other's work, and engaging in conversations that benefit the industry as a whole. I hope that, as you continue to work in this industry, you strive to engage and build the community as well. By doing so, you can contribute to making email marketing a discipline deserving of respect, instead of the ugly cousin of web design.

I hope you learned a lot while reading this book. I learned a lot while writing it. Please keep in mind that, though I have spent a lot of time designing emails and exploring best practices for effective email design, I do not know everything there is to know about email design, and the techniques discussed in this book are not gospel. There are a lot of talented email designers using a variety of approaches for the various issues discussed in this book. None of them is necessarily the right approach, and none of them is necessarily wrong. I encourage you to play around with your designs and your code. Keep experimenting and testing out new ideas. I look forward to seeing what some of you come up with next.

I am shocked at just how often HTML emails don't validate when I check them. Not validating your code as you go is the best way to end up in pretty hot water. I highly recommend getting very comfortable with the W3C validation service. I use Chris Pederick's Web Developer Toolbar and run its 'Validate Local HTML' command so often it's not funny. If anything is going to go wrong with your email that relates to structure, the validator is going to find it first.

Nicole Merlin
Email Wizardry

References

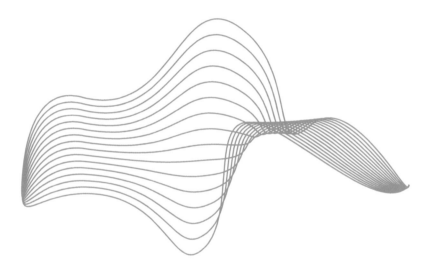

I could not have written this book without building on the work of others in the email marketing community. It is a shame that the community is relatively small, fragmented, and quiet. I hope that this guide will contribute to remedying some of that. The following is a list of resources used both while writing this book as well as in my day-to-day practice as an email designer.

Email Service Providers

Campaign Monitor
campaignmonitor.com

My favorite ESP. They have a beautiful and robust platform that makes it easy to attract subscribers, send them great emails, and track the results of your campaigns.

MailChimp
mailchimp.com

Another popular ESP. They provide an excellent product, a great free tier, and valuable resources for getting the most out of your marketing.

Emma
myemma.com

Create and send beautiful emails more quickly and easily with our foolproof drag-and-drop email creation tools. Better yet, make sure they get seen with Emma's industry-leading 98% deliverability.

CakeMail
cakemail.com

Another excellent option with pre-built templates, an advanced template editor, and good pricing options.

ExactTarget
exacttarget.com

Built for higher-volume sending and the enterprise, ExactTarget has a suite of tools for larger campaigns.

There are a ton of others including larger companies like Silverpop (silverpop.com), Constant Contact (constantcontact.com), BlueHornet (bluehornet.com), and Bronto (bronto.com). Shop around and find which email service provider provides the tools you need.

Tools

Sublime Text
sublimetext.com

Every designer needs a text editor. Sublime Text is my favorite. Easily customized and extended. A lot of people like WYSIWYG editors like Adobe Dreamweaver, but when working with responsive emails, I think a text editor + browser for resizing is the best option.

Mozilla Firefox
mozilla.org

My browser of choice for designing. The developer tools "responsive mode" is one of my favorite tools. CTRL+SHIFT+M on Windows or CMD+SHIFT+M on Mac to view your responsive email.

Web Developer Extension
chrispederick.com/work/web-developer

This extension for Firefox and Chrome adds amazing tools to inspect your design and code. Use the built-in validation tools to quickly find problems with your code and structure.

Litmus
litmus.com

The best testing tool for emails. View your design in a variety of browsers. Testing tools for plain-text, colorblindness, subject lines, and spam filters. They even have an interactive mode to troubleshoot code problems.

Email On Acid
emailonacid.com

Similar to Litmus but with a few different features.

RIOT
luci.criosweb.ro/riot

Radical Image Optimization Tool for Windows for compressing your images before sending.

ImageOptim
imageoptim.com

Similar to RIOT but for Mac users. It's always a good idea to optimize your images before sending.

Bulletproof Buttons
emailbtn.net

Generate bulletproof buttons for your email campaigns with this tool from Campaign Monitor's Stig Morten Myre.

Bulletproof Backgrounds
emailbg.net

Also from Stig, this tool helps generate better support for background images across clients.

Litmus Scope
litmus.com/scope

Litmus has a great bookmarklet and tool for seeing how other designers code emails. A great way to get a closer look at advanced techniques.

Guides To Email Best Practices

Campaign Monitor Guides
campaignmonitor.com/guides

Campaign Monitor has a number of well-written guides packed with information on topics ranging from designing emails to getting in the inbox. A great resource to learn more.

Will It Work?
campaignmonitor.com/resources/will-it-work

Campaign Monitor has a slew of resources for learning about support across clients for a variety of techniques and solutions.

MailChimp Guides
mailchimp.com/resources

A great collection of guides about both the practice of email marketing as well as guides on MailChimp's service for different types of clients.

MailChimp Research
mailchimp.com/resources/research

A nice selection of reports from MailChimp with some hard data on a variety of topics.

Email Standards Project
email-standards.org

The Email Standards Project works with email client developers and the design community to improve web standards support and accessibility in email.

Blogs and Websites

Campaign Monitor Blog
campaignmonitor.com/blog

Campaign Monitor shares information not only on their products, but also email best practices, community champions, and great email designs.

MailChimp Blog
blog.mailchimp.com

More of a focus on MailChimp products but still a fantastic resource for information on best practices and marketing techniques.

Litmus Blog
litmus.com/blog

The folks over at Litmus post some great case studies on emails, as well as company and industry news. I love Justine's video updates on client usage, too.

Email Wizardry
emailwizardry.nightjar.com.au

Nicole Merlin's excellent blog on everything email related. She shares some killer insights and techniques to make the most of your email designs.

Email Design Review
emaildesignreview.com

Elliot Ross of Action Rocket blogs about email design, tips and tricks, and best practices.

STYLECampaign Blog
stylecampaign.com/blog

Anna Yeaman of STYLECampaign fame posts some of the best articles on everything email. Her Responsive Email Design video is a must-watch.

Email On Acid Blog
emailonacid.com/blog

The team at Email On Acid provides some great insights into the design and testing process.

Inspiration

Campaign Monitor Gallery
campaignmonitor.com/gallery

An extensive gallery of killer campaigns. My go-to for email design inspiration.

Beautiful Email Newsletters
beautiful-email-newsletters.com

A massive collection of email newsletters from all sorts of companies. You could lose yourself in the collection for days.

HTML Email Gallery
htmlemailgallery.com

A great collection of designs as well as resources for learning more about email design.

Email Gallery
www.email-gallery.com

Similar to HTML Email Gallery - showcases a lot of newsletter designs.

For a more comprehensive list of resources, visit the *Modern HTML Email* resources page at http://resources.modernhtmlemail.com.

I would like to express my gratitude to those who helped me during the process of writing this book. Thank you to Ros Hodgekiss, Anna Yeaman, Nicole Merlin, Justine Jordan, Elliot Ross, and Alex Ilhan for their contributions and insights; Campaign Monitor and Litmus for use of their services in sending and testing emails for the book; and my wife, Valerie, for her support and help with editing.

Jason Rodriguez

rodriguezcommaj.com
@rodriguezcommaj

Made in the USA
Lexington, KY
09 July 2014